ANCHOR BOOKS

WEB OF THOUGHTS

Edited by

Heather Killingray

First published in Great Britain in 1997 by
ANCHOR BOOKS
1-2 Wainman Road, Woodston,
Peterborough, PE2 7BU
Telephone (01733) 230761

All Rights Reserved

Copyright Contributors 1997

HB ISBN 1 85930 567 9
SB ISBN 1 85930 562 8

FOREWORD

Anchor Books is a small press, established in 1992, with the aim of promoting readable poetry to as wide an audience as possible.

We hope to establish an outlet for writers of poetry who may have struggled to see their work in print.

The poems presented here have been selected from many entries. Editing proved to be a difficult task and as the Editor, the final selection was mine.

Web of Thoughts is a traditional collection of poetry written by poets from all walks of life; from housewives to civil servants and from factory workers to the elderly.

The poems in this collection reflect the poets thoughts, feelings and convey messages which you and I can relate to.

Web of Thoughts is an inspirational book of verse, with an insight into today's modern world.

I trust this selection will delight and please the authors and all those who enjoy reading poetry.

Heather Killingray
Editor

Contents

Ribbons Of Dreams	Annette Jones	1
Autumn	Katherine Averis	2
Persephone	Clare Dyas	3
The Allotment	Tyron Allbright	4
The Things That We Do	Alan Green	5
Pilgrimage Of Faith	Barbara E Stubbs	6
Timeless Thing	Richard Clewlow	7
Butterfly (For Dawn)	Barrie Howard Evans	8
Lives Of Unloved Wives	L J Povey	9
Body Politics	Sharon Marshall	10
Mother's Day	Dennis Turner	11
Morning Glory	Ian Barton	12
A Lonely Girl	Prince Rhan of Kathari	13
To The Cat That Walks Alone	Aniseed Chadwick	14
Mary Of Whithnell	Barbara Sherlow	15
Little Boy In A Garden	Linda Blakey	16
Feed The Machine	Gary Parker	17
Digging	David Hazlett	19
I Long To Share	Julie McKenzie	20
A Special Wish	The Western Dreamer	21
From Me To You	Helen Nelson	22
Beach Party	Sheila Waller	23
Untitled	P Allen	24
Midday Break	Pauline Haywood	25
My Mother	E Edwards	26
Kids	David Sheasby	27
Stand-In	Jean Freeman	28
In A Moonlit Cask	Michele Glazer	29
My Best Friend	Jean McLaughlin	30
The Thinker	Wilf Allsopp	31
The Pheasant	Shaun Hillen	32
Leonard Percy Hart 1925-1997	Mark Redgewell	33
Nagging Mums	Elizabeth A Williams	35
Plastic Cup	Linda Adam	36
Midsummer	Ann Dulon	37
Cobwebs And Thorns	Clive Weston Sirett	38

Title	Author	Page
A Redundant Teacher Told To Sweep Leaves	David Crossland	39
Sean's Robin	C M Bellamy	40
Inspirations	E B Holcombe	41
Granma	Elizabeth Skidmore	42
Taylor	Theresa Hartley	43
Got Their Number	Kim Montia	44
My Night Poem	Ryan Martin	45
Your Dreams Are All Images	Michael Spittles	46
The Only Hope Left	Jan A Krupa	47
Success	William Price	48
All My Yesterdays	Terry Daley	49
Cosmos	Ruth Purdy	50
A Cosmic Address	Edward Graham Macfarlane	51
Memories Of Life On A Stud Farm 1920-1926	Harry Bye	52
A Bear	Carol Gilby	54
When It Rains	Melvyn Roiter	55
Requiem For Dimple	B J Poskitt	56
A Letter To Santa Claus	Lucy Carrington	57
Autumn Poem	Desirée Ask	58
Mer	Jennifer Polledri	59
A Death	Joe Hughes	60
Robert, It's Me	Janet Rose Marsh	61
Untitled	Hazel Yates	62
The Bird Table	Betty Green	64
Blame	Danielle Turner	65
Burning Witch	Jill Coles	66
Today And Always	Stephanie Bones	67
A Parable For Today	Joy McCall	68
No-One At All	Margaret King	69
Surf Your Dreams	May Strike	70
Katie	Patricia Ware	71
Today's Misdeeds, Tomorrow's Curse	Michael Chappell	72
The Instructor	V Davies	73
Kiss Of A Stranger	Penny Verney	74
Silence Is Golden	Ruby-Ann Okker	75

Hong Kong Air	David Bennett	76
Success	Hannah Birch	77
A Winter Night	Eadie Logan	78
Granny's Line Dance	A J Don	79
Thoughts	Hayley Edwards	80
Sorry - Gone!	J M Hefti-Whitney	81
Divine Love	Caroline Gill	82
Untitled	Luana Dogwiler	83
What Was Your Game?	Rukeiya Patel	84
Twilight	Mary Cornelius	85
To Be Seen And Heard	Kerry Pickett	86
Heartache	Alice Porteous	88
A Garden Welcome	N B Mason	89
Clinging	K Larcombe	90
Fear	Colin Patrick Jennings	91
What The World Admires	R Kelly	92
Lily Of The Valley	Sara Baldwin	93
Today	Gladys C'Ailceta	94
Pictorial England	Gerald Aldred Judge	95
Glory	Henry Charles	96
The Greatest Betrayal	Joan Isbister	97
A Day On The Farm	Alex I Askaroff	98
The Carp	Daniel Evans	99
Natural Progression	Dennis Malin	100
You . . .	Alison Berridge	101
Rattling Vultures	Parry McDaid	102
Voices	Jenny Campling	103
For Zoe	Pippa Hartley	104
Saturday Night Fever	Win Cottrell	106
I Want My Mum	Juliette Dorkings	107
The Spectator	D Davis-Sellick	109
Dominic	Sylvia Watt	110

RIBBONS OF DREAMS

Friends talk, while strangers pass by,
oblivious to their good graces.
The conversation rains laughter
on the dismal, clouded, skies.
Words - a prism of colour,
float effortlessly on the breeze,
and eyes dart,
amid friendship's gaze.
A moment of time,
caught in the webbed maze, of familiar dreams.
Will the strangers still pass this way,
- or catch the ribbons of dreams
and become friends too?

Annette Jones

AUTUMN

Bright mornings, frost-shadowed and blue-skied;
The sunshine warms the last apples on the tree.
Come and enjoy it while we may
For winter will soon be here.

See the high hills are a patchwork of brilliance,
Orange, purple and bright green among the rocks.
The woods are woven with colours
So varied and beautiful.
I want to keep them
Touching my memories through the cold winter.

A windy day sets the leaves flying
And soon they are thick on the damp grass
Among the scattered nuts.
The sunlight shines through bare branches
And the squirrel hurries away as I approach.

The garden bonfire with smoke curling
Brings fragrant promise of the warmth in our home.
Dusk falls; let us go in,
But, as we pass by,
See the white rose, shining in the twilight.

Katharine Averis

PERSEPHONE

Biting into non reality
A void completely,
This woman
Who dreams
Of death and dying
Lies so sweetly.
She for whom spring
Of little flowers
Bursting into bud,
Is the regeneration
Of yet more blood.
So still she lies,
Her heart slow to question
The eternal thread,
That reaches through tomorrow,
Towards the dead.
She stands in vehemence
Born on the underground
And pulls her shawl around her.

Safe and sound.

Clare Dyas

THE ALLOTMENT

a plot of land of your own, a good old-fashioned way
fruits of your own labour, to take home as your pay
children helping parents, the way it should be
a down-to-earth knowledge, a start of charity
children getting married, babies on the arrive
wolves at the door, the knowledge of survive
fresh air and exercise, to meet the body's needs
watching plants of the land, grow from little seeds
hours of creative pastime, working on the land
a day out for the family, what could be more grand
fresh fruit and vegetables, fit for a king
new friendships blossom, from a basic thing

Tyron Allbright

THE THINGS THAT WE DO

What gives us the right
To do the things that we do
We are destroying the planet
Both me and you
We pollute the rivers
We pollute the seas
We kill the meadows
We kill the trees
We murder the whale
The elephant too
It's a disgrace
The things that we do

Alan Green

Pilgrimage Of Faith

I flew across the sky to Israel the place of Jesus' birth
a land as troubled now as it was then.
I stood on the site where the angel came to Mary
in the town where Jesus grew to be a man
I touched the star in the manger
where the wise men and the shepherds came
and looked on the well in Cana
where he turned the water to wine
wandered by the Jordan where John the Baptist reigned
and travelled in the wilderness where once Jesus came.
I sat on the shore of the Sea of Galilee
and imagined I saw Peter in his boat upon the sea
I walked on The Mount and in Gethsemene
where ancient olive trees had witnessed his awful agony.
my mind saw the city as it was in Jesus' day
and silently I stood in the tomb where once his body lay.
Now the stories in the Bible have a picture in my head
making them more real every time I hear them read.
But there isn't any need to travel so far
to see all these wonderful things
For Jesus is with you wherever you are if only you'll let him in.

Barbara E Stubbs

Timeless Thing

you're so sad as
you have come back
none of you are wanted
if you do not like it
here anymore get out
creeps like you can
all go off into
the one long oblivion
a timeless thing that
would so sort of last
would stand so apart
from all the rest
of the consequences that
are so there in life
the council all said
no to you and that
was so hated by you
even now you hate
your day is up
go sweep the roads
you low-down cheat
all your family are
only a bunch of nuts
who are freaks without
any sort of ambition
no matter what job
any of them will do
the ones with the streak
that smells of hate
at the skill of others

Richard Clewlow

BUTTERFLY (FOR DAWN)

A breach is made;
your chrysalis cracks.
Encroaching moonlight
reveals the beauty within.
A hurricane of beating colours
destroys the fragile and tedious hide.
Solitary confinement is over,
the excited water-colour is free.

Away from your natural unnatural prison,
your lifetime flutters past in minutes -
hypnotic vibrations of the wing.
A technicolour panorama passes before your eyes.

An age of hibernation, dormant
and safe in the darkness,
is forgotten in a second of you
rainbow energy and love,
silhouetted against the sun.
Yet your eclipse has vanished in the beat of a wing.

Barrie Howard Evans

LIVES OF UNLOVED WIVES

I gazed outside from my windows within
I softly crept away
as the years rolled down my chin
Damp, moistened rivulets of pain
they in sorrowed silence dripped gently.
Locked up here in your ivory tower
Beauty kept hidden from their desire
Like a seed that blooms
Buried deep in fertile soil
It's a sin if I spark their fire.
So here I stay dormant in my dank surrounds
Slowly suffocating, wilting,
suffering in silence.
A misty maiden
Hazy,
Hidden behind her veil
like a shameful secret too shy to
reveal to the rest of the world.
Hopelessly shrouded
for fear of your discontent, or
jealous greed.
Forever a shadow
forever a seed.
Never allowed to be what I am
break forth from the cruelty of a man
To bloom, to be seen as me
a glorious orchid, a rose, a tree, the beauty.
The power, the passion all freed
if only I wasn't crushed by a weed.

L J Povey

Body Politics

I could build cities from your skin
And line up culture along the veins
And ligaments and wrap every
Reluctant surly star
Pulled from its slow orbit
And there would be language in
My song my voice racing from
The old silence I will not
Retreat this night I dare yes
I dare and all the more loving
And warmer still warmer
I do not halt the pulse
Or calm the rising pant
Or soothe the beat
No smooth bed for we storm-rovers
Your blood beneath my nails
And my skin beneath your heat
Do you love this body
Falling and rising in sleep
And like erotic politicians
We pull a string of endless questions
Me from you
You from me.

Sharon Marshall

MOTHER'S DAY

I know today is Mother's Day
The one day of the year,
Apart from on her birthday,
I should *really* show I care;

But just this once I must confess,
Although it's very hard,
That on this very special day
I didn't send a card.

It's not that I'd forgotten her,
Or meant to be unkind,
It's just that I had something
Rather pressing on my mind.

I'm sure that she'll forgive me
For no card upon her shelf.
For on this day I've just become
A brand new mum myself!

Dennis Turner

Morning Glory

Newspaper footsteps
Walking in a dream
Easing my way
Into the day
My throat is dry
From the night before
I'm floating on a Typhoo shore

This life I will glorify
But first I must get the sleep
From out of my eyes

The toast is burning
The kitchen is on fire
The smoke alarm is singing
The alarm bells are ringing
I sit and drink
Another cup of tea
I'm floating in a haze
When I should be making history

This life I will glorify
But first I must get the clutter
From out of my mind
Then the morning glory will be mine
The morning glory will be mine

Ian Barton

A Lonely Girl
(In dedication to Sylvia, my wife, my life)

Oh! There she stands, a lonesome girl tears streaming down her face
A true beauty of anytime who took life in her stride
Today in the Plaza her thoughts are elsewhere
She waits to see the Pontiff himself
For her faith has weakened, no longer strong
Her hope lays with him to help her troubled soul
Inside tormented her mind torn with grief
Finding no rest from her own belief
Tears stream from her eyes, her hands never still
At long last a door opens and she is welcomed in
A cardinal directs to a small room, and bids her wait
Minutes later to her joy the Pontiff enters
And she kneels to kiss his ring
She pours out her soul explaining why she is troubled so
He smiles down benignly into her eyes
Gently he says, 'Once I experienced just the same
So many many years ago, before I wore this holy crown
Go back into the world young lady, you have no shame to bear
No matter what we do in life God forgives us all'
This time as she left her head held high, she walked tall
A love glowing inside her heart
she had never known
A gentle smile had spread across her face
Her spirit lifted way up high
No more tears, her face now completely dry

Prince Rhan of Kathari

TO THE CAT THAT WALKS ALONE

I dream of gazing from a hill
Upon the house that may not still
Contain what's loved and sorely missed
Will years condemn we only kissed
A part of life the hurried meeting
Bad habits that we kept repeating
Too far away and yet you touched
What was there but never clutched
That cry for love those hapless pleas
Emotions only hindsight sees
In a car and peering down
Upon what's now a fallen gown
Beside the church led to our walk
Rose-coloured memories of a talk
I'm sure you smiled and held the hand
Of he who failed to understand
The reason why two souls in need
Could only watch each other bleed
Christmas was a broken time
The fool commits the perfect crime
Too late for tears let raindrops fill
A memory - with the wipers still.

Aniseed Chadwick

MARY OF WITHNELL
(Dedicated to friend, Mrs Mary Webb of Withnell)

Mary and I we've been friends
Nigh on thirty years,
Thoughtful, salt-of-the-earth she
Never leaves me in tears.

Especially since my accident
Nineteen ninety-four,
When almost whole of life on
Me, went and closed its door.

Mary has stood by me yes
Through most thick and thin,
Keeping vital company
She helped me keep up my chin.

Mary's the practical
Whilst I am the 'dizzy',
But respect for each other
Keeps the two of us busy.

Not in each other's pockets
Can't call us Darby'n Joan,
She seems to sort of sense when
Sometimes I feel alone.

She turns up with some cabbage
Broccoli and spuds,
Like Red Riding Hood she brings
All of my favourite goods.

Barbara Sherlow

LITTLE BOY IN A GARDEN

'Who made all of these flowers, mom?
And who made all of these trees?
Why have the birds got no arms, mom?
And who made the colour of peas?

Why is that fly sort of shiny?
How did that frog get in there?
Why is a ladybird tiny?
Why is a pear called a pear?

Who said that this is a weed, mom?
Who makes the butterflies dance?
How will that grow from a seed, mom?
Why are there thousands of ants?

Who do we thank for this fruit, mom?
Who do we thank for the sun?
I really do like all these worms, mom.
They look like they're having some fun.

When I'm a man, I'll grow flowers, mom.
When I'm a man, I'll grow trees.
Then you can come in my garden.
Will you come, mom? Will you, please?'

Linda Blakey

FEED THE MACHINE

Jesus saves in neon blue,
Synthetic love and urban rule.
As a post box smoulders in the street,
Drivers rubber-neck the obsolete.
Fluorescent light entices a fly,
Electric spark catches my eye,
Meat on a spit slowly rotates
And above from a window pours
        A little drum and bass.
Knowledge is power
And power control,
And that's all you need
To process a soul.
Hail the bar-code
And the god of greed,
As I'm looking for change
To feed the machine.

TV cameras scan the streets
In infra-red and body heat,
Gargoyles stand at a nightclub door
Searching all the men and smiling at the whores.
A holiday poster shows the Barrier Reef
And a postcard underneath, for instant relief.
Fluorescent light entices a fly
Only this time I see it die.
Knowledge is power
And power control,
And that's all you need
To process a soul.
Hail the bar-code
And the god of greed,
So get on your knees
And feed the machine.
Heed my warning one and all,
A simple message for king and fool,
Bar-code money

Bar-code food.
Bar-code head
Bar-code you.

Gary Parker

DIGGING

The spade goes in
though there is a reluctance
no cross to mark a place:
It's just at face value
removing the first
cut scoop of topsoil;
you hit a stone or
bone or nasty root
and something snaps:
a bad vibration
through the fingertips
to the brain, which
is only jelly - believing
there is no gain without
pain. The belly throbs
with exercise it's not
used to - and when
the trouble starts it's into
clay and through, a
heavy ochre cold but
wet. One
could make pots of
gold with this.
And yet only two spits deep.
Already thus - infinite possibilities
begin to seep:
What's covered up
on moon landings
And hid beneath the deep.
Each stratum then reveals.

David Hazlett

I Long To Share

Once we shared the laughter
and we shared the tears,
And we shared the friendship
down throughout the years.

But now you've gone
and time's moved on,
I've changed and so have you,
It's very sad don't you think
after all that we've been through!

I long to share with you again
the laughter and the tears,
And all we've ever been through
together throughout the years.

A friend I've lost but still I hope
that we will meet again,
Some day up there in paradise
our friendship we will mend.

And for all eternity we'll be together
and make up for lost time,
Our friendship never again will wither
for the sake of 'Auld Lang Syne'.

Julie McKenzie

A Special Wish

A wish for special happiness to you, from me
a loving wish from my heart for you, every single
day, I can't explain this love I feel coming from
within my heart, reaching out to you, overflows
from my heart to you.

A wish for special happiness in all kinds of
ways in every day that passes by, that special
wish is within me for you, that each day over-
flows with my love for you coming from within
my heart, reaching out to you, overflows from
my heart to you.

My special wish to you from me in this heart of mine,
a loving light to light the darkness, coming from within,
my heart reaching out to you overflows from my heart
to you.

A wish for special happiness we two share my prayer
in a world of turmoil and strife, my love with warmest
thoughts lights the way, for such a special reason, to
a very special person for a happy time in our life, love
coming from within my heart, reaching out to you love
overflows from my heart to you.

A wish for special happiness may each day that follows
my darling know in truth and certainty, my love has not
faltered nor changed, it's there for you alone love coming
from within my heart, reaching out to you, love overflows
from my heart to you.

The Western Dreamer

From Me To You

(A little girl writes to her grandmother)

Dear Grandmother
It comes but once a year
The stage my only fear
Seated in the first ring
To you I will sing
My first jingle
My first single
It's our annual play
I hope you will stay

Yours Clair

Helen Nelson

BEACH PARTY

The clouds are high, drifting by
Sun is warm and the sea is calm
Today we'll party and have fun
Folk lying on the golden sands
Others dancing to the band
Children playing, running round
Sand castles looming up
Let's all yell and shout!
Balls bouncing to and fro
Feet jumping high and low
Picnic baskets brimming full
Lots of drinks keeping cool
Jump the waves on the shore
Shiny wet pebbles by the score
Have a swim if you dare
Smell the salt in the air
Everyone's having fun
Right until the end of day!

Sheila Waller

UNTITLED

On my
        bed
Again
The rain
On the
        window
Pane
Autumn
        in school
Found me
        a fool
The love of the rain
The love of the pain
Autumn in school
On the window again.

P Allen

MIDDAY BREAK

Playing outside with
The things that they like,
Digging in the dirt
And squabbling over the bike.

They have been on the swing
And up and down the slide,
They had so much fun
It was a job to get them inside.

They are both asleep now,
Though it's the middle of the day
They've worn themselves out
With a hard morning's play.

Better not disturb them
Just let them be,
Enjoy the peace and quiet,
And have a nice cup of tea.

While they are resting
We dare not make a noise,
We talk in whispers
As we pick up the toys.

Just check they're all right,
They look so cosy and warm,
But we know it's not for long
It's just the quiet before the storm.

Pauline Haywood

MY MOTHER

'Mother', you can see the love in the name
Nothing she's done to bring her fame
She works, cooks and cleans from morning till night
A lovely fire what a welcoming sight
The children arriving home from school
It's homework first, that's the rule
Dad breezes in with a little kiss
He's never yet been known to miss
Mother we love you for all you do
There's no-one in the whole wide world like you.

E Edwards

KIDS

I have two little horrors,
they live with me each day.
Sometimes they are very helpful,
and other times get in the way.

The house is very peaceful,
when they go out to play.
I have to keep my eyes on them,
that they'll never go astray.

'I want, can I have,'
are things we often hear.
But when they cannot have them,
they'll often shed a silent tear.

Sometimes they are nice to know,
and will behave themselves.
And can be very useful,
when I clean off my shelves.

David Sheasby

STAND-IN

Please don't call me mummy, when you ask to hold my hand,
Please don't call me mummy, for you don't understand,
Please don't call me mummy you'll only break my heart
Please don't call me mummy, for soon we'll have to part,
I am just her stand-in, till then I'll always be,
Your stand-in mummy darling, you don't belong to me,
I've walked the room, paced the floor, till tiny teeth came through,
I've held your hand for those first steps, till I let go of you,
Now you're back where you belong, to start a life that's new,
I pray to God you don't forget the things I've taught to you,
With all the love that I could give, perhaps a little more,
In passing years you'll hear this poem and know who it was for.

Jean Freeman

IN A MOONLIT CASK

Like a candle in the darkness
Stirred by each mood of the wind,
I will sensually equate each murmur of ocean
With the beat of your heart.

I saw that esoteric ship slope past
When your feelings were enmeshed in my bones,
Wooden with silver lights, augmenting
The promise of the moon.

How will I induce you to hold destiny's hands
When you slip onto a diverted path;
Psychics, astrology or divine intervention?
It hurts like a needle
Plunging into a boil!

Will we escort the heirs of the Montagues
And Capulets . . . hardly a curtsey
Or bow to earth's symphony,
Before bonding, ebbing eternally?

The galleon spectre reappears with a cask
Furrowed by veins of moonlight;
It is our time now, we dare
Not evade our fate; your heart
Pulsating with mine in a moonlit cask.

The flares of Her Holy lighthouse
Elating our path . . .

Michele Glazer

MY BEST FRIEND

Jean is the name of my best friend
To me she is the best.
The worries I have shared with her,
No-one could ever guess.
She always seems to find the time
To listen to my troubles
although Jean is my best friend
she is best friend to others.
She can tell if I am feeling down
I don't have to say a word
She knows just by the way I walk
I know this seems absurd.
No matter how many friends I have
She will always be the top
For she knows what she means to me
for we've been through a lot.
She has a heart that's full of good
and she never could be mean
Now that's the kind of friend I have
that's my dear friend Jean.

Jean McLaughlin

THE THINKER

His thoughts are usually so profound,
His mind continually going round,
He thinks of death, he thinks of life,
Of love and hate, of war and strife.

Religion often comes his way,
Do we believe? Should we pray?
When will we find the answers to 'why'?
Possibly only when we die.

Wrestling with thoughts,
His whole life through,
Into old age,
Wishing he knew.

So the man who's the thinker,
Goes struggling on,
While his next door neighbour's
Thoughts are none.

Wilf Allsopp

THE PHEASANT

What a pleasant bird is the pheasant.
Much too elegant to be called a beast.
His meat is beautifully nutritious and
makes for a wonderful feast.
And with this game lad, never a dull
                          moment is had.
A good sort by all it is thought,
Never ferocious or even precocious
                          when bagged.
By God what a marvellous sport.

Yes, what a pleasant bird is the pheasant.
His temperament second to none.
Persuading him to take to the sky
gives our beaters a great deal of fun.
But when the pheasant's at his most
                          pleasant,
Is when it's in our direction he soars
And we catch his elegant contours in
sight of our twenty twelve-bores.

Shaun Hillen

LEONARD PERCY HART 1925-1997
(40TH COMMANDO REG'T ROYAL MARINES 1942-1946)

When I was a boy, he'd swing me high through the air,
Bite my earlobes and tickle and tease till I screamed,
I remember the smell of his pipe-smoke, and that big wide grin,
He'd always be there for us, or so back there it had seemed!

In 1942 he had joined the Marines, only 16, he'd lied about his age,
And at Anzio and Rome, he'd faced the tyrant Eagle and all of its
    rage,
But together with his comrades, they'd checked the retreat to its
    alpine nest
So that little boys could shriek and laugh! And Europe at peace
    could rest.

He was the first man to shake me by the hand! When I'd tried to
    kiss him goodbye aged eight,
He'd said that as I was nearly grown up, and a big boy now, we
    ought to set this thing straight!
He was the biggest and straightest of men. A spade always got
    called just so!
And how the world keeps turning without him? I still cannot quite
    say I know!

For we buried him last Monday, in a green English field near
    Northampton.
Which is he'd once informed me: 'A hundred miles from the
    nearest sea!'
What better place than at her heart for him, that once struggled to
    keep England free!
Six old comrades in green berets, their medals and shoes gleaming
    in June's bright sun,
Familiar ground this for them, here to say farewell to a friend. To
    bury another good chum!

An old soldier bugle in hand, colours flying in the breeze begins the
                                          poignant 'Last Post'
His face is purple, veins set to burst! Those lungs are not what they
                                          were, all those fifty years ago.
When together they'd danced, with the dangerous mistress called
                                          fate. At that place they call Anzio!
Oh! Play bugler play! Though I know it's harder for you now than
                                          then. Play for those that went there
with you, but never came home again! But most of all play it sweet,
                                          and play it for my Uncle Len!

Play so clear that you cover my tears! So the world doesn't see how
                                          I bend, and am blind with the pain.
But most of all, play it sweetly for him, that has gone from us now.
Until we all meet him again!
And he'll never swing me high through the air, nor chew my ears,
                                          or tickle and tease till I scream,
But if this poem finds heaven: know that you're very well loved!
And very much missed!
And always welcome in all of our dreams!

Mark Redgewell

NAGGING MUMS

Have you washed and scrubbed your face?
Have you tied your undone shoelace?

Have you brushed and gelled your hair?
Have you changed your underwear?

Have you taken your vitamin C?
Have you turned off that TV?

Have you been doing the ironing for me?
Have you been making the daily cup of tea?

All the things you do for me
Will be worth it later on, you'll see.

Elizabeth A Williams (8)

PLASTIC CUP

The people standing in line,
waiting, moaning, everything lost!
He sits alone, this child, on the earth,
watching, perhaps wondering,
all his possessions by his hand
a plastic cup, on an upturned can.

The people slowly disappear,
unknown to him, the silver bird,
snatches them, flying to another land,
and still he sits, with his
plastic cup on an upturned can.

Did anyone notice him?
How shall he face this evil,
that drives people from his land?
Too young a mind for poisoning
too innocent for fear,
and patiently, sitting in the sand
with his plastic cup on an upturned can.

Linda Adam

MIDSUMMER

It is now the time at Stonehenge to be,
All the hippies gather there, feel free,
New-age travellers, come and they chant,
Around the stones, now it's banned, they can't,
What wrong did they do? No harm was done,
Wait for solstice, rising of the sun,
Something mystical just being there,
Through contemplation, being aware,
The sun rises beside the stone heel,
Shone into the middle, warmth feel,
Spiritual feelings are close to you,
With its longest day and that's so true,
Stonehenge a temple, the Druids say,
More north you go, the longer the day,
Folklore, myths and the legends of old,
Men ran through fire, so we are told,
Girls practised magic in the twilight,
Husbands to be, revealed at midnight,
Shakespeare wrote a Midsummer Night's Dream,
Fairies, madness and lovers redeem.

Ann Dulon

COBWEBS AND THORNS

Tread softly past the old man
Asleep in the hedge,
Where cobweb shreds of hope
Still cling lightly to . . .
The thorns of his experience.

From time to time he jumps
In cat-like sleep,
Remembering tadpole jam jar trips
Across those fields of green,
And the first time he kissed Jenny
From number seventeen.

He came home from the war
In a grey flannel suit,
And was happy for a while
Delivering flowers in a van,
Until the young upstarts all came running
With their energy and fun,
Soon he lost the battle
He thought he should have won.

One day . . . someone who was close to him
Will take a day off work,
Hire a skip and throw away
All that is left of his eventful life,
A broken chair . . . mouldy loaves of bread
Behind the cupboard doors,
Tread softly past these shreds of hope
One day they could be yours.

Clive Weston Sirett

A REDUNDANT TEACHER TOLD TO SWEEP LEAVES

angry thoughts embittered cup
miss dismissed such rotten luck,
serving novice probation term
students would not work to learn.
you cannot impart learnéd knowledge
so offer hands in other homage,
not hidden, cold, revengeful love
supplicant winter lost summer above.
we coloured frozen frosted all
leaves in measured season fall,
shedding half-recalled regrets
in gardens gathering benefit debts:
a million rejects dress forest tree
fallen beauty swept up by me.

David Crossland

SEAN'S ROBIN

Where do robins go in the summer?
And where do the primroses hide
For so much of the year?
Do the robins disguise themselves as sparrows,
Putting on dull grey coats,
Perching on park benches, begging for crumbs?
And how do they lose their dignity
With such success and conviction?

Maybe they hide in those holes in trees
Where the branches used to be,
Just beyond our vision.
They are never found dead on a road
Like pigeons, starlings or crows.
How strange!

Perhaps they are figments of our wintry imagination,
Their appearance marking the coming of winter,
Their departure the end of spring,
Is the robin no more than that?
This precise and gallant little bird.

Maybe his first appearance in the branches,
Inaccessible and alluring,
Is like the first winter
Dropping upon the world, like a frosty cloud.
And his lifespan is measured in imagination,
And not in years.

C M Bellamy

INSPIRATIONS

I get my inspirations
As I lie upon my bed
Of all the things I've done
And all the things I've said.

Of all the friends I've had,
All through my life
And even of the man,
Who took me for his wife.

And of all my children
Who have gone away,
I don't expect I'll see them
Until my dying day.

But oh what a wonderful life it's been.
I'm afraid to awaken
In case it was a dream.

E B Holcombe

GRANMA

Granma's house is full of books
she's not as silly as she looks
when she says 'No' I know it's so
not to touch, where not to go

Granma's hair is grey and straight
when I am there I stay up late
then into bed ready for a story
about the world and all its glory

Granma's eyes are brightest blue
they always know the things I do
if I'm naughty or do things wrong
she may get cross but not for long

Granma's house is always full
with lots of people never dull
Granda says she'll talk forever
will she forget me? Oh no, never

Granma's house has quiet times
if I could I'd make them mine
to have her hug and hold me close
for it is the time I love the most

Elizabeth Skidmore

TAYLOR

Whoops
Sorry
I didn't know you were there!
Even though you follow me everywhere!
I'm so sorry, I do really care
You should have been called Shadow,
Every time I turn around you are there!
Still, it's nice really
'Cos, I know that you care.

Theresa Hartley

GOT THEIR NUMBER

As little individuals
This nation's youth are blessed
Free to grow and blossom
With no need to feel oppressed

Guiding all our children
As an elder brother does
The governmental waspish stings
Preceded by its buzz

All little individuals
And so to each a gift
A unique number helping
To identify them swift

Schools will soon all echo
Uniform numeric bliss
'Pupil 1439 Smith!'
'Oh yes, I am here Miss!'

Kim Montia

MY NIGHT POEM

Night is a dark shadow
I see a round moon
I hear a squeak from above
The stars are like flying diamonds
The moon is like a shining ball
Night is bedtime.

Ryan Martin (9)

Your Dreams Are All Images

Your dreams are all images
Like the clouds floating upon a summer sky
And as you watch them drifting with each new breeze,
You see them all changing like the drifting sands of time.

Michael Spittles

THE ONLY HOPE LEFT

Hail Mary, full of grace; won't you take
a look at this place? Now don't think Mary
I'm having a go, but there's a few things
here I think you should know.

The man I saw the other day, started to cry
then went on his way. He's nowhere to go -
a life on the street. I'm a bigger sinner
than he'll ever be!

Hail Mary, won't you shine on me? I've just
seen a couple walking down the street. They're
both hand in hand and laughing and gay, but it's
difficult to live when you don't feel this way.

I'm not alone, this I know, there's millions of us
swimming to the same shore. So if there's a reason
why this way is this way; I really would like some
kind of answer today.

There's so many crosses and it isn't just me. It breaks
my heart when I look around and see. The girl who's on
drugs, the life on the game; and at the end of the day, it's
really all a crying shame.

Is that all I see? Is it all rubbish? Is this really all that it is?
Still, at the end of the day, I'm glad it's been OK;
I think of the people who are really alone, and I
thank you for my happy home.

Jan A Krupa

Success

Success is speaking words of praise
In cheering other people's ways
In doing just the best you can
With every task and every plan.
It's silence when your speech would hurt
Politeness when your neighbour's curt.
It's deafness when the scandal flows
And sympathy with other's woes.
It's loyalty when duty calls
It's courage when disaster falls.
It's found in laughter and in song
It's in the silent time of prayer
In happiness and despair.
In all of life and nothing less
We find the things we call success.

William Price

ALL MY YESTERDAYS

I remember well when I was young
How it was in an age now gone
Though my eyes dim, still can I see
Vanished images so dear to me
Childhood pleasures while always at play
Somehow it seems the sun shone each day
Simple and innocent were we all
Building dens or kicking a ball
Up in the mountains the air was clean
Beauty all around could be seen
Climbing in trees and home-made swings
Through the air, as if we had wings
Trying to catch fish in river or streams
Acting out the heroes of our dreams
The season's harvest we would gather
Blackberries, nuts and many others
Simple pleasures, simple games we'd make
With only a hoop or just one skate
A weekly trip out to the cinema
With some sweets, were a joy forever
Shielded from the world by our parents
Without fear, wherever we went

Terry Daley

Cosmos

'Tis said our earth was a scrap of flotsam
Sent hurtling into space,
Spinning, spinning 'til it slotted
Into its allotted place,
To join the dancing planets
Round the sun, which gives us light,
Following the moon
Which illumines darkest night.

And in the icy realms of space
The stars shine way up high,
Though many light years will have passed
Between their twinkle and our eye.
Orion and the Pleiades
And the filmy Milky Way,
The Plough and Venus glow all night
To disappear by day.

We know the moon's not made of cheese,
There are no men on Mars,
And the planetary craters
Are just old volcanic scars.
They've investigated Saturn
And probed its moons and rings
No longer can we speculate
And dream about these things.

In spite of astronomic science
And all it may attain.
We hope some of the magic
And mystery will remain.

Ruth Purdy

A COSMIC ADDRESS

Friends and fellow humans,
We should all agree to be,
Creators of a single state
For *one humanity.*

We have come out from the jungles,
Out of caves and down from trees
But we may have *a brilliant future*
If *cosmic planning projects* please.

We need a *'human persons' project,*
To confute the killing cults
And a *Glasnost Global Corporation,*
To spread the *free-debate results.*

Part-world projects are mistaken
Whether Scot or Brit or ethnic breed,
Religious or materialist.
All have personal choice of creed.

The cosmos is *enigmatic,*
This is our *'basic agreed fact',*
At least that's how we'll view it,
When *globalization* we *enact!*

Edward Graham Macfarlane

MEMORIES OF LIFE ON A STUD FARM 1920-1926
(Memories of Plantation Stud, Exning, Newmarket)

Every morning it is a lovely sight
Racehorses passing with their colours so bright.
As we make our way to school each day,
We stand back and let them go on their way.
Those stable lads have legs more like matchsticks,
They canter along our favourite walks
There are several horses quite a long string,
The lads are quite happy, some of them sing,
They were up early just after the break of day
Grooming, mucking out and bringing in hay
They will be galloping on the heath for a while
The trainer will watch as they complete the mile
We live on a racing stud farm where there are mares and foals,
Where there are loving paddocks, not disturbed by moles.
Young fellow with barrow clears up all the muck,
Wheels it away, it is filled to the buck,
The mares and foals take their daily graze,
Sun shines through clouds with its gleaming rays,
At 4 o'clock the stud hands come out,
Halters in hand, horses know what it's all about.
They shout 'Come on,' horses run to the gate.
Halters on now, they are led away for their bait,
To the horseboxes they go, clean lovely and bright,
Horses then fed and bedded down for the night,
The male horse is stabled away from the mares,
He's taken out sometimes, where he goes to, nobody cares.
Sansovina is the name of that stallion racehorse,
The Derby he won on that Epsom racecourse.

In the evenings, when the paddocks are clear,
We play football, and cricket with our makeshift sports gear,
It's lovely living on a stud farm,
If you behave you will come to no harm,
It's seventy-odd years since I lived there,
I pay it a visit when I have time to spare,
Things have changed a lot over the years,
But the neigh of a horse one always hears.

Harry Bye

A BEAR

A bear went out fishing.
He caught a little fish.
He held it in his paw,
over a large dish.
Ten minutes he sat looking,
at its silver sparkle,
and then he gently took it,
and returned it to the stream.

A bear went on looking,
at the bubbled fish,
as it splashed its fin,
in the shimmering stream.
Free at last, turning right round.
It swam away, to a safer place.

A bear went on home.
To his small cave,
eating honey from a large pot.
'Yum, yum,' said bear.
'Now my honey's all gone,
it's time for me to go to bed.'

Carol Gilby

When It Rains

When it rains
When it rains
When it rains
I do not care
When it rains
When it rains
My thoughts I want to share
When it rains
When it rains
It doesn't make me wild
It's no different how it was
When I was a child
Some things never change
Some things more positive
When it rains
As life goes on
I just want to live
When it rains, each spot
It means so very much
Each spot that falls upon me
I just want to touch
Each drop that falls upon me
As when I sing a song
It makes me wet
And makes me feel
So very, very strong.

Melvyn Roiter

REQUIEM FOR DIMPLE

The scoop of earth in which you lay
Is now no longer warm, and chill the grass.
Not that spot wherein, on summer's day
Reclined at ease you watched me as I toiled
Among the flowers.
Or, sleeping, let the daylight pass
In idle hours.
But not without some small caress
From you to me to show me that you cared.
It was not needful! I could guess
All that you could not say in human tongue
Before you left.
Seven happy years we shared
Now I'm bereft.

In Memoriam.
Your daily contacts all will disappear
Your earthly body with this earth will blend.
But, while I work outside, I'll feel you near,
Because, for seven years, you were my friend.

B J Poskitt

A Letter To Santa Claus
(Dedicated to HRH Diana, Princess of Wales.)

Oh Santa dear, it is so delightful to see you here
around on Christmas cards once more, so jolly and cheerful,
dashing in a sleigh drawn by a herd of fleetfooted reindeer.
As this inspires me with a wonderful idea
for the most thrilling Christmastime.

Santa why not conjure up magic and give us a sleigh ride
on the Holy night to the fairytale land of Christmas far away
with hills mantled with white sugary snow, where lofty green fir
trees, adorned with silver rime grow, and on a crisp morning
a robin trills so fine, so bold 'A Merry Christmas to you all'?

It would be even greater fun if you could take us around
your mystical, full of crystal splendour grotto,
festooned with diamond rainbow-like icicles,
resembling fairy lights and twinkling star-like chandeliers.

But to experience a Christmas in all its glory and cheer
treat us to the greatest merriment of all:
make us happy, joyful, so enthralled
that we could sense we have lost all track of time
to be awoken not earlier than the New Year
with a brighter future to unfold!

Lucy Carrington

Autumn Poem

Winter's late this year
Still hang the leaves green and gold,
Some lie thickly on the ground
But on my lilac tree
The tiny buds of spring are found;
But as life goes further on
The strains of pain prolong,
We see the beauty of the dawn
In a baby, stable born.

Desirée Ask

MER

A monumental structure standing on the desert sand,
The most stupendous work of human hands.
From the polygonal base to the apex in the sky,
A noble Tomb protruding from the sands.

The sloping sides, triangular, a burial tomb for kings,
Concealing wealth and riches, precious gems and other things.
A treasure trove obscured, as the clouds that hide the sun,
Preserved for all eternity - remote from everyone.

What mysteries lay within these walls of ancient granite stone?
How many slaves have lived and died, each one of them alone?
The sands released, the blocks they fell, the slaves went to their death,
In chambers, sealed, no passage of air, they uttered one last breath.

To be with Pharaoh at his side, in this world and the next.
No choice was given to the slaves, their destiny was set.
Those whining souls within the Tomb, their fate they did not know.
But a future life of splendour hailed the favoured King, Pharaoh.

The sacred ibis from above looked down upon the King,
Surrounded by the shrikes and doves, with brightly coloured wings,
These giant crystals, centuries old, stand bold for all to see,
But the spirits from within those walls . . .

                              Oh, who will set them free?

Jennifer Polledri

A Death

Now half blinded and unable
To make his way around alone.
He was dying, it was night time
In this psychiatric home.

A vicious man who was quite able
To strike you hard and dangerously.
They told me as a student nurse
Make sure and watch him carefully.

But now his life, it ebbed away,
His time on earth near through,
I held his hand for those last hours -
An action I would never rue.

He had seen the Prohibition,
The Great Depression and the Wars.
He often spoke of his adventures
In his cute Chicago drawl.

But now he lay forlorn and friendless,
Adrift from family and home.
He clutched, held hands so eagerly
Until his life it was no more!

Joe Hughes

Robert, It's Me

Like a bird you fly so
Swiftly by;
Up above the deep blue sky.
I call out
'Robert please look I'm over here,'
You turn the corner
And disappear,
No backward glance do you give,
I wonder, do you know
I really live!
Forever out of reach
Forever out of sight, but
Forever in my dreams at night.
I pray one day
You'll stop to see,
The one who truly loves you,
Robert,
It's me.

Janet Rose Marsh

Untitled

I wish I'd have let you
converse
instead nervously
my voice trembled,
out words tumbled, and jumbled
pure nonsense.
But not witty Jabberwocky.
I spoke ten to the dozen.

Are you with another
who's all ears
calm and cool?
As I sit here silently
soulfully. Dolefully. Bereft
isn't it a shame?
For a while I smiled
when you came.
Then I wondered what the
next time would be like,
after you left.
I listened.
Every moment of it
rewarding.

So lonely.
So unadvised a host
a ghost of a person.
Who never existed
till you rang my bell.
Getting so sick.
Now I'm well.

Well, looking forward
to your return.
Yearning for more
words
I was learning
without realising
when you kissed me
goodbye the temperature
started rising.
As I did spiritually
to heavenly bliss.

Hazel Yates

The Bird Table

Many little birds visit our table,
One looks up quickly when they hear a squabble.
It wouldn't be nice for them to hurt one another,
Then you notice it's babies trying to decide who should go
next to mother.

Usually we get only the tit family,
But this year we were visited by woodpeckers - three.
We had often seen them in the hedge,
Or nestling on the window ledge.

Dad and junior are the most handsome of all,
But mum also plays an important role.
Their colouring is red, black and white,
And they are very grand when they spread their wings in flight.

We saw dad, feeding from the fat ball,
But he passed a morsel down - to be shared by all.
Mum received it and baby was fed,
Then they departed, I expect to be tucked up in bed.

Betty Green

BLAME

I got the blame
So I had to run away
Far from where
I could be found
Live my life
Afraid and alone
Always wondering
If anyone had known.
I tried to run
But I couldn't hide
The guilt was
Eating at my insides.
Couldn't face another day
My life was worthless anyway
It was quick
But not painless.
I knew I had to suffer
But now as I lie in peace
I feel a great relief.

Danielle Turner

BURNING WITCH

I plunge my hand into the flames
Quite fearlessly.
Comprehension of terror is beyond me.
That smell, acrid, choky - that is myself
And particles of my ash
Are inhaled by my nostrils.
I hardly remember a time when I was not
Aware of lapping fire, smoke circling.
These do not matter to me.

What hurts my heart,
Makes this a grief to me,
Are the raptures of these people, their manic shouts;
These agitate me.
Their condemnation, censoriousness
Seem uncalled for.
I was not wayward, nor wilful.

Why is my suffering a boon to you?

Jill Coles

TODAY AND ALWAYS
(Dedicated to my husband Ken)

Hear me whisper
        hear me shout.
                Hear my words -
                        as they flow out.

See me happy
        see me cry.
                See me fondly -
                        with your loving eyes.

Feel my joy
        feel my pain.
                Feel my heart -
                        pulse through my veins.

Share my nights
        share my days.
                Share my life -
                        today and always.

Stephanie Bones

A Parable For Today

Early in the morning,
Unable to sleep,
I wandered to the end of the garden
And stood at the fence
Overlooking the sheep-field.

The farmer's boy was filling the food-bins,
And had reached the third one
When it dawned on the sheep
(They aren't quick)
That food was available.
The first few sheep to reach the bin
Were followed in order by all the rest,
All at the same bin, jostling
And climbing over one another
To get food.

Two other bins, overflowing,
Stood untouched in the field,
And though I watched for a long time,
No sheep approached them.

So, I see that there are two ways:
The way of the crowd,
Anxious and fraught,
Competitive and unmindful;

And the way of opportunity,
Imaginative and reflective,
Solitary and far-seeing;

Where the struggles end
And the dreams begin,
And where food-bins
Are always full.

Joy McCall

NO-ONE AT ALL

I miss her every day
There's no-one to say
'Give me a cuddle'
Or throw me a ball
No-one at all.
I listen to her voice
Is she in the hall?
Or can she hear me bark?
I do it in the dark
When I'm dreaming.
Still, I listen for her call
But there's no-one there
No-one at all.

Margaret King

SURF YOUR DREAMS

Ride high the waves, surf on your
Dreams, live your life, don't delay,
Don't leave your dreams
For another day.

Scale the heights, ride the wind,
Live your dreams now today,
Don't let them crumble and decay.

Time goes by so quickly, unnoticed
In life's rush
For we are here but for a moment.
And before you know, it's too late
And your dreams are all but dust.

So live for today, don't scatter your
Dreams by the wayside,
Ride high your dreams, don't let them
Go unseen.
Then you won't weep tomorrow for
Thoughts of what might have been.

May Strike

KATIE
(Dedicated to my niece)

My precious little Katie
When you were only four
Jesus came a-calling, knocking at your door

With eyes so blue and hair so blonde
The Lord he knew where you belonged
Little angels weren't meant for this earth
God knew this when he gave you birth

We love and miss you very much
But you have felt his tender touch
God in his mercy has his way
And in his arms forever you will stay

So up in heaven Katie look down from above
Look on us all with God's great love

My precious little angel
With eyes so blue and hair so blonde
God knew where you belonged
So one day when time has passed
We all will be together in heaven
At last

Patricia Ware

TODAY'S MISDEEDS, TOMORROW'S CURSE

The fur trade is back, is nothing now sacred?
A thought for those animals killed to be worn,
Millions of dollars, are spent in this market,
Endangered species taken, what will be next?

Clinically killed in an atrocious way
So their skins are kept clean, what an awful shame,
Wake up to reality, time is running out
If we don't act now, it will be too late.

Today's misdeeds will be tomorrow's curse,
Life is cheap to us now, what a terrible place,
Empty reserves, are like trees without branches,
And the buffalo no longer roaming American prairies.

Baby seals are butchered, taken from their mothers,
Remember one day we shall answer to another
For all our misdeeds in killing off nature,
Our environment should come first
And not left to cry over.

Michael Chappell

THE INSTRUCTOR

On the first day he called
I thought what a handsome man
Till I saw the car
It looked like an old tin can.

You will teach to drive in that heap of junk
Then expect me not to flunk?
Oh my dear he said with a little smile
We're only going a few mile

Well into the car I got with a puff
I did the mirror and all that stuff
I took off the brake
Now he said you must concentrate

Now this is the way you go round the bend
I said that's not hard with you my friend
He gave me a look of despair
By this time I didn't care.

My first lesson I remember it well
The instructor thought he'd been to hell
He asked if I planned any more
As he was making a dash for the door.

V Davies

KISS OF A STRANGER

Why did it ever
have to end?
The feeling from
that kiss still
sends,
shivers running
down my spine.
That kiss again I
shall never find.

Why did he have
to go so soon
and leave me with
such morning
gloom?

For this stranger
who once I've met,
gave the sweetest kiss
I shall ever get.
A kiss so gentle
sweet and soft,
but now this man
for me is lost.

I'm not in love
no way,
not me,
attracted yes but love
would be,
not for him but for
his kiss.
Which to receive again
would be such bliss.

Penny Verney

SILENCE IS GOLDEN

Silence is golden, I guess that this is true
But sometimes it's right
To speak a happy word or two
Greeting one's friends
Giving a word a cheer
Saying you love someone
Whom to you is dear

But sometimes idle chatter
Is just a silly mask
When really one does not have to speak
To say what's in one's heart
So if you do not always hear
The things to you - that you hold dear
Remember *Silence is Golden.*

Ruby-Anne Okker

HONG KONG AIR

Hong Kong has freedom's clutch
Foreign rule has peaceably ended
The legacy of eighteen forty-one
Since imperial Britain claimed it
Took the colony until July's year
Nineteen hundred and ninety-seven

Fireworks a laser would envy sparkle
Against the city's congested skyline
Of tall lit buildings bathed by neons
Reaching China's firecrackers in air
As Britannia's sublimely-lit figure
Leaves harbour refuge forever

China's golden port is released
With sadness and dignity
One country two systems basic now
Hong Kong changes the dragon's tail
Oriental leases expired as agreed
Successful Taiwan is another island

Hong Kong though unique is tough
Finance and commerce its core
Art and movies centre's food
With reflections its constant breath
Legal freedoms bring nerves
China's completeness is one and two

David Bennett

SUCCESS

Why should we give up doing poems in writing
When there's so many words that's exciting?
Give them a chance for getting through
Words in poem I am sending to you

Acceptance comes when having done our best
Along with others they are under test
Encouragement plays a special part
Stirs that something within the heart

Pen moves along the writing paper
Imagining things, God and the Saviour
Should this be a winner for opening a door
More work will be coming this for sure

Poem's expression is coming to its end
Patience a virtue this one I do send
Hoping for something this to gain
Work all in all speaks of things to remain

Success is something for singing about
Brings out the best in us no doubt
Words run on bringing out satisfaction
Good or bad there's a sure reaction

Hannah Birch

A Winter Night

Darkness is closing in
I don't care. All doors are closed.
I curl my toes into the sheepskin rug
soft and warm from the heat of the fire.
Outside the wind wails.
The flickering light from the television
dances on the red carpet. I am cosy.
I must draw the curtains against the night.
Outside the wind wails.
Bare branches on a nearby tree
are clawing to reach the warmth, but
they can't escape their earthbound trunk.
Even though the wind wails.
Soft white flakes are battered
into the tentacles. There is ice in the air.
Outside the wind wails.
Tomorrow morning the now-flaying branches
will be encased and still.
There will be no escape.
Tomorrow they might weep and sigh.
I draw the curtains.
Inside there is light and warmth.
Outside the wind wails.

Eadie Logan

GRANNY'S LINE DANCE

Grandad told the story,
It was a real nightmare
When Granny did her line dance
Rocking in her chair.

She did her entertaining
In slippers with furry trim
Swaying to the 'western jive'
And twisting every limb.

Granny had a drink or two
And maybe even more
Then she jumped out the rocking chair
And boogied round the floor.

She had a good old knees-up
Doing 'grapevine' to the right
And when she did a twirl about
The poor old cat took fright.

Granny thought she was clever
Threw down her walking stick,
Then she glided around the room
And did a great high kick.

The music was still playing
But Granny wasn't in time,
They were doing forty steps
Whilst she was doing nine.

She puffed and panted a little
Said the 'pop' had gone to her head
So Grandad took her walking stick
And chased her off to bed.

A J Don

THOUGHTS

Everybody has them,
Good or bad.
Thousands come a second,
They can drive you mad!
Long or short,
Fast or slow,
Some can be high,
Some can be low.
Help us appreciate them,
Not to be misguided,
If we just think hard enough,
We will not be undecided.
The control centre of dreams,
The control centre of thoughts.
Special things,
So I think we ought,
To encourage and develop,
The precious gift of thought.
If we develop the habit,
Of always using our mind,
The world itself may enjoy,
The things that thought can find,
Delving deep into a forgotten past,
Like ghosts haunting that will forever last.
So don't forget what we can do,
If we really really want to.
I have tried to develop my thoughts,
And share them all around.
And it is my sincerest wish,
That pleasure may abound.
To my fans and readers,
Wherever you may roam.
I hope that I may find you,
Enjoying my latest poem.

Hayley Edwards (9)

SORRY - GONE!

The note was pinned to the outside blue door for all to see
Sorry - gone!
But where, when, why? So I'll explain, well at least try.
I'd sat by the telly pen in hand to chuck me lottery card in the bin.
One. Two. Three. Four. Then five and to my surprise number six!
I'd won the lottery! Me eyes were staring, transfixed!
I took me suitcase from under the stairs, heart going like the clappers,
Why did I need to pack? I could buy anything I needed, I'm going crackers!
I phoned my daughter, then my sons, for them like me our lives had now begun.
I didn't sleep, I watched the clock, planning my debut into the unknown world of the rich, I'd get a new frock!
Financial advisers, bank managers, now almost smiling looked after me brass,
But I'll not put all me eggs in one basket, well, I'm a Yorkshire lass!
I went on a cruise to faraway places, palms and all that sort of stuff,
Azure seas, silver sands, images of that 'Family Robinson' in my mind,
I'd lost two stone in weight! In my sarong I looked like Dorothy Lamour!
I hires a stretch limo to ease me feet for a dramatic scenic tour,
I'm tanned, I'm supple, I've learned to snorkel!
I look at the whopper diamond on my hand and chortle!
My villas in Tuscany, France, The Riviera of course, an apartment in 'Paree'
Well I did warn you all what I would do didn't I? You didn't believe me!

J M Hefti-Whitney

DIVINE LOVE

To know you is to love you,
To love you is never feeling alone,
To have you is being the luckiest one,
To lose you would be hell on earth,
To face a dawn without you by my side would
Mean never again a smile, only tears,
My heart would pour out tears of blood,
My life would no longer be,
My heart would wither and die.

Caroline Gill

UNTITLED

Moon, rising copper
on shimmering shores growing
gold in your shadow.

Luana Dogwiler

WHAT WAS YOUR GAME?

You rolled the dice and the game began
Rolling the dice you got six, I got one
I moved a step but you didn't follow
It seemed one empty game board, making it hollow.

You started the game wanting to win
All you proved was that 'love is sin'
How could you roll the dice and move when you wanted to?
I wasn't prepared to wait and see who loved who.

You wanted to fold the game board and put it away
But I wanted to carry on playing it safe
It was so easy for you to play this game
But tears came from me with grieving pain

Before I knew someone else was rolling the dice too
Your desires were set wanting someone new
You moved ten steps ahead leaving me behind
In front of me you made yourself blind.

Just what was your game, I was so foolish not to see
I feel sorry for her who's waiting to move on step three
The game you play will hit you back in your face
Embarrassment will strike and the world won't be a pretty place.

Rukeiya Patel
from Blackburn

TWILIGHT

Come twilight adrift before night.
A peaceful time removed from day,
All those distinctive things from sight,
In the hours of darkness will stay.
From the beginning man of old,
Lay down to rest and ponder,
Watching shadows becoming bold.
Distant hills to cloak with wonder.
Outstretched, spread at nature's command.
Meeting night with its pale moonlight,
Covering earth as sea bed - the sand,
Certain and secure as is its right.
What powerful source of faint light
Closing the day to welcome night!

Mary Cornelius

TO BE SEEN AND HEARD

It seems that because we're young,
Things we say and do are wrong,
Therefore we never have a say,
Which leads to problems of today.

Adults say we 'don't know we're born',
That statement's such a yawn,
Because the rubbish that they spew out,
Doesn't explain the violence about.

Children are walking down the streets,
With knives and guns instead of sweets.
Adults say 'Hooligans!' and that
Their parents propriety.
Not blaming, of course, the state of society.

Because us children don't have a voice,
For some, guns are the only choice,
To be heard amongst older prats,
Who, in their day, never encountered indecent acts.

Deceit, murder . . . it's all we know,
Because older generations have let the world go,
Us youths have had to grow up fast,
Instinct and survival have helped us last.

The wars have done but more battles remain,
Equality, age, colour, what will we gain?
What will happen when all tears have been shed?
What will happen when all blood is bled?

What future have we if things all go to pot?
When we die of global warming, rape, a bullet shot?

Adults don't know they're born or know the likes of strife.
They haven't long to go, we've just begun our life.

Who will mourn and weep for us?
The spirit of an aborted foetus?

Kerry Pickett

HEARTACHE

The staring at nothing -
The flutter inside oneself, not knowing why
Withstanding the utter quietness
Of the world around.
Although the birds are there
And yes - somebody passed by
A black jacket - and an arm
Around another human being
Quiet laughter -
Not resented, but feeling
A deep pain inside, wrecking
The dull ache already there -
Who am I to be begging
A deity to let me go?
Go where? To another lonely place?

Alice Porteous

A Garden Welcome

Have you ever been aware of one's
place in a garden. For instance
to hear the gentle rustle of leaves.
The beckoning of branches.

Giving a welcome to one's own
garden paradise. Sit awhile and
savour the beauty all around you.
For you are rich indeed.

To be near to occupy such blessings -
which one could call one's own -
available to such delights in your
very own garden, day and night.

The flowers of all kinds,
shrubs and trees forming
a background to such beauty,
all giving one a real welcome.

Come and sit awhile for such
a garden is here for the taking
of pleasure indeed, and are here
to say. We are all here to lighten up your life

You are the gardener we know.
May we say thank you for all
the loving care you give to us all.
For without your loving care things
would not have the same loveliness.

Thank you Heavenly Father for the sunshine
and the gentle rains, which make my beauty
a bit like your own Glory.

N B Mason

CLINGING

As the ivy clings to the garden wall
I cling to you, my love, my all
As the ivy spreads so my love for you
Grows stronger each passing day thro'
No matter what each year may bring
To you my love I'll always cling
Thro' rain or shine
You'll still be mine
I'll cling to you while life shall last
Till all our days are safely past
And when we reach our final rest
May leave with heavenly possessed
And reach at last the final shore
Where all is peace for evermore.

K Larcombe

Fear

Oh. Saddened fury, oh whiff of fear
Oh tautened nerves caused by family dear
Oh lonely nights in search of sleep
I lie enracked in darkness deep
I spend my days with worrying
My thoughts gone wild and hurrying
Through my mind go scurrying
        These saddened thoughts

And never will I ever learn, nay,
My thoughts of fear to you I pay
Please hear my plea and drift away
These lonely days and nights I yearn
Away from fear's merciless burn
I spend my time in search of a quiet day
        And leave me peace

What price I pay, what cost a lease
Still search do I
For sanctuary in quiet peace

Colin Patrick Jennings

WHAT THE WORLD ADMIRES

What the world admires
As excellent valuable and good
God really didn't intend
That they should

He gave clean air
To breathe
Land and sea
Plants to grow
Friends to know
All this so free
Along with love
For you and me and family

Material wealth
So unspeakably mean
When balanced with the wealth
Of the soul unseen.

R Kelly

LILY OF THE VALLEY

You are a raindrop you are the sun
You were my first light, when my life had just begun
You were my strength when I was weak
You were my voice when I couldn't speak
You are my hope you are my song
You always saw the right when I thought I was wrong
You are my smile when I'm feeling sad
You always saw the good even when I was bad
You are my angel you are my friend
You always give me a cuddle with your arms to lend
For all I want is to see you happy
For you are the spring, the lily of the valley

Sara Baldwin

TODAY

I can't write, I can't draw,
I don't seem able to do anything at all
Yesterday it seemed so easy
I was bright fresh and breezy
Why is it some days all goes well
Then the next day can be hell?
Life has its ups and downs
Some days there are no bounds,
Nothing is perfect is it though?
That's the way it seems to go
Usually my thoughts I get to rhyme
I am finding it difficult this time
In front of me is a beautiful rose
Her delicate perfume reaching my nose
Isn't it a pity that the stem she adorns
Has to be covered with prickly thorns?

Gladys C'Ailceta

PICTORIAL ENGLAND
(For Floyd)

A poetic view
Of newly fallen dew,
A tearstained field
Of twinkling stars,
Undermined by petrol fumes
Of passing cars,

Plastic bags
Caught in hedge and brier,
Broken bottles,
Discarded old tyre,
Overhead a celestial choir,
The dawn chorus perched
On telegraph wire,

A picturesque estuary
Glistening
As it catches sunlight
After rain,
Soiled from the discharge
Of sewerage drain . . .

Gerald Aldred Judge

GLORY

It matters not what we do what we think or care
It is a fact we can't deny I am here and you are there
Trying to be so different from what was meant to be
Gives life a mighty challenge the life of you and me
Stand back and bite the bullet the clarion cry of some
With the bullet stuck between our teeth the answer's just begun
Through life we are shepherded by those whom we enlist
To find they are no different from us whose arm they twist
Red green or blue or yellow it matters not a jot
Whatever taste we favour there's still that other lot
Don't kid yourself you're different no matter what you wear
What matters if you're rich today tomorrow's always there
Just strength and trust life asks of you to see what it can find
When you have found Valhalla think of all you've left behind

Henry Charles

THE GREATEST BETRAYAL

I see the hurt that's lurking in your eyes,
I feel your pain, twice magnified in me,
A pain you'd like to hide from me, but then,
I helped to put it there.
I see the evidence of what is not,
What might have been.
You open up the longing in my soul.
You bring before me all the arid years,
Too dry for tears.
I've heard it said you can be very kind,
You have so much to give,
You give so much,
To those who matter to you now.
Allegiance newly forged.
Perhaps one day you'll understand the pain,
You'll know betrayal from a child,
One you had thought your own.
As now you've chosen how you want to be,
Your love is not for me.
I know, of course, I'm in the wrong again,
But that is hardly new.
That's where I've always seemed to be to you,
And you have cause to be dissatisfied.
Much of your past leaves me no room for pride.
I hope your new commitments serve you well.
As to regrets, only the years will tell,
All things concluding, where did they begin?
You've left me on the outside of your life,
But, never fear, I won't be looking in.

Joan Isbister

A Day On The Farm

Windmill sails cutting the harvest air,
Heavy horse resting without a care.
Grain a-grinding, husks gently falling,
Sweat on Father's brow, skylark calling.
Late morning breeze scented with flowers,
Dad works the land for endless hours.

Field mice scatter from the scything blade,
Mother's setting our lunch in the shade.
Yeasty fresh bread and lumps of ripe cheese,
Buttered scones with honey from our bees.
Swifts swooping, soaring, darting, diving,
Hop fields of bronze the country thriving.

I'm just soaking up this summer day,
Too young to help I'll be in the way.
While Father's busy piling the straw,
Chasing field mice is my only chore.
Dilly and dallying all day long,
Whistling a tune or singing a song.

Patches on my shorts, mud on my face,
Hair in tangles all over the place.
Poppies swaying beneath a blue sky,
The moist warm earth, Mum's blackberry pie.
Dad silently eating, time rolls on,
And all too soon our paradise gone.

Windmill sails cutting the harvest air,
Heavy horse resting without a care.
Grain a-grinding, husks gently falling.
Sweat on Father's brow, skylark calling.
That summer day safe in memory.
With Mum, Dad and their little imp - me.

Alex I Askaroff

The Carp

I was sitting at the pondside,
Watching my float bob around,
When I felt a tug on my rod,
It pulled me to the ground.

The carp shot off in the distance
It flew off to the reeds,
I didn't know what to do,
Help me, help me please.

On hooking such a big one,
I couldn't believe my luck,
Ten pounds or maybe even more,
I'm glad I read that book.

Eventually I got it in,
All the hard work done,
Now that I could have a rest,
I'd eat my jam-filled bun.

Here I come John Wilson,
So watch out Johnny boy,
I will be your follower,
In catching carp and koi.

Daniel Evans

NATURAL PROGRESSION

The theme behind this little rhyme
Is Mother Nature and Father Time
To make our earth a place to love
They must work just hand in glove
One gives us the time, the hours
The other gives us veg and flowers
One gives the welcome spring
The other every living thing
One gives us sun to melt the snow
The other time for things to grow
Mother Nature gives us birds and bees
Rain and wind plants and trees
Father Time gives us time infinite
Sixty seconds to every minute
Mother Nature moves both day and night
Father Time gives dark and light
Mother Nature needs both time and space
To reproduce the human race
Flowers and animals to increase
Father Time will never cease
Every day each leaf and flower and feather
Let's hope they always work together
'Cos if they should ever drift apart
Where would time end and nature start?

Dennis Malin

You...

You are everything to me.
You are my security blanket,
My ID card,
My keyring.
I am attached to you.
You are my fireside,
The warmth of my bed,
My friendship band.
You have my heart,
My soul,
And my mind.
You are my shoulder to cry on,
My arm to hold on to,
My body to embrace myself.
You are everything to me,
Which is why I have to leave.

Alison Berridge

Rattling Vultures

They stand . . . somehow (although stationary)
like sharks circling at a shipwreck,
eyeing alike the 'warned' and the unwary,
as victims slip from GPO's greasy 'deck'.

No conscience mars predatory programme -
they'll 'devour' money you may need;
extent of penury doesn't mean a damn
to the parasites who'd thrive as you would bleed.

They only feed upon the weakened prey,
prowl not outside the *workers'* den,
but stalk the unemployed on each 'giro day',
striking as their quarry seek to leave the 'pen'.

Single-minded, they thrust a plastic box
at each happy head which dares to show . . .
This is why collectors are shunned like the pox
even though it be a charity well-known.

Perry McDaid

VOICES

What is that noise?
Why it's voices in the hall
Up I get from my chair
The grandchildren have come to call

Three little girls, one little boy
They laugh and play so funny
They bring me such a lot of joy
It's worth much more than money

There's Terri with her big brown eyes
And mischievous little Abby
Quiet gentle Jefferson
And tiny baby Daisy J

Who would have thought
When first we met
That you would leave me alone
But you were ill, so Jesus called you home

You have left me a legacy
No, it isn't a lot of money
But three small girls, a quiet boy
They make my days so sunny

So darling when I sit alone
And hear their little voices
And hold them gently on my knee
It is just as if you are here with me

Jenny Campling

FOR ZOE

I had a very special child -
Even though she could be wild!
She had such a lovely face,
Was slim and had a certain grace.

Although she's gone, I can see
Those naughty eyes following me -
'It can't be true! It can't be true!
I want to hold and cuddle you.'

Why did you have to go,
Especially when I loved you so?
We shared so much, didn't we?
Now, what will become of me?

I still talk to you -
I laugh and cry with you;
I know that you can hear
Because I know that you are near.

Remember how we laughed and laughed
When we decided to be daft!
Looking back makes me smile,
You really were a special child.

Remember how you used to say:
'Cheer up, mum - please be gay!'
Now, whenever I feel down,
I can see you start to frown.

I try hard not to be sad
And think of all the fun we had.
But sometimes when I sit and think
Tears roll down as I blink.

I miss you so much, my little love,
And don't understand why God above
Chose to take you when he did . . .
Was there a dreadful skid?

Please, God, take good care of you,
Until I can be there too.
Heaven has now been endowed
With my very special child!

Pippa Hartley

SATURDAY NIGHT FEVER

I think I've caught a fever, it's called 'The Lottery'.
Last week I got two numbers up but not my number three.
The week before I got two more, let down by legs eleven.
This week I'm banking all my hopes on lucky number seven.
There's really something wrong with me, for when I say, 'No more!'
They give the blessed jackpot out, I feel I've got to score.
And then I dream of all the things that I would like to do.
Get out the card just one more time and cross off number two.
It's almost eight o'clock at night. Quick switch to BBC!
I'm getting really hot again, this time I'm sure it's me!

Win Cottrell

I Want My Mum

It's my first day at school
My uniform is all crisp and clean
We all lined up in the big school hall
I don't know anyone
I can't help but cry
I want my mum!

Playtime is fun, playing games
'Let's play kiss chase' cries Sheri
Running fast round the yard
I fell and grazed my knee
I can't help but scream
I want my mum!

School exams
My stomach is in knots
I can't think straight,
everything's a jumble
I can't help but mumble
I want my mum!

My first job
Who will I meet?
Will they be friendly?
Will I sit alone?
How will I find my seat?
I can't help but think
I want my mum!

The day I moved out
We had tears in our eyes
As I pulled away I heard
'I'm only round the corner'
But these words rang in my head
I want my mum!

There never goes a day
when I can't help but
Scream
I want my mum!

Juliette Dorkings

THE SPECTATOR

There is a body of opinion that deplores
What's become known as factory farming;
And when I saw a farrowing sow locked in a cage
That fitted like a glove, not harming

Her perhaps, but making of a living, breathing
Creature, an object suitable only
For breeding, in a most efficient way, I knew
The system'd gone wrong somewhere. This lonely

Sow expanded in my mind, until it blotted
Out the summer afternoon, and I'm
Again standing beneath that ancient tree, a dumb
Spectator, as in that other time.

D Davis-Sellick

Dominic

The moment I saw him I knew,
No words passed between us
And yet on that night,
My feelings for him grew and grew.

Would he care as much as I cared?
Would our lives run along
On parallel lines?
Would our hopes and desires be shared?

He was all that I'd longed for and more,
His hair was dark brown
His eyes deepest blue
With a face anyone would adore.

I had to believe that he'd love me,
There was no way of knowing
But still I was sure,
Our love was just meant to be.

As I looked in his beautiful eyes
I knew I felt something
No other could feel,
It had taken me quite by surprise.

I had to be certain, be sure,
If he didn't love me
If he didn't care,
The thought shook me right to the core.

I had lain my heart on the line,
As I cuddled him closely
I knew instantly,
That the love of this child was mine.

Sylvia Watt